THE TRUTH ON THE TONGUE

Geoffrey Heptonstall

Several of these poems first appeared in these anthologies:

Yellow (*Jambu Press*, San Francisco) ***Voices Unbound*** (University of Pennsylvania).

Elemental Water, (Pembroke College, Cambridge) ***100 Poems for the 21st Century*** (*Rough Diamond Poetry Journal*) ***Made from Midnight*** (*Poets in the Pines*)

Other poems first appeared in *As It Ought to Be*, *Penn Journal of Arts & Sciences*, *Poetry Catalog, Poetry Super Highway, Quill and Parchment* and *The Seattle Star* (USA)

Littoral, Northampton Poetry Review (UK)

ISBN: 978-93-6354-853-4

First Edition: 2025
Rs. 200/-

Cyberwit.net
HIG 45 Kaushambi Kunj, Kalindipuram
Allahabad - 211011 (U.P.) India
http://www.cyberwit.net
Tel: +(91) 9415091004
E-mail: info@cyberwit.net

Printed at Repro India Limited.

Contents

ORIGINS

Origins are immersed in innocence
with secondary meanings,
the written script being nuanced.
I can see this for myself.
Resembling chaos on recollection
comes a narrative of attainment,
changing when the order is revised.

The perhaps of it invites contact
were the signs legible.
A close reading would be all,
the fallen fruit well flavoured,
Eyes upon the lineaments of desire,
a landless sea of the setting sun,
the perception of her approaching.

WAKING THE DREAM

On waking the dream may live
with open eyes to the world
that imagines itself
to be the one reality.
Another is preserved by the power
to impress on the mind.

Our thoughts on this
are free to defy gravity
as they drift homeward to the stars.
Observations of motion concur
with the ancestral acceptance
that the earth is fragile.

ANGELS

And a wiser sun rises.
to complete the circle.
Harmony makes a certain return.
There are signs of ravens
in cloud-like shadows
passing through the clear sky.
All gifts of innocence
abandoned in the womb
when the spirit casts its spell
on those who fear a portent
will betray them to the world.

Then there shall be angels.

THE NARRATIVE BEGINS

As the hour approaches
in never ending style
he sees what nobody knows.

There is always a curiosity
on a throw of a dice.
from one who chances everything.

He follows, drawing a conclusion.
In there he will tell his tale
that goes down to nowhere.

Someone steps on the stair,
she who make her escape
watching those who come and go.

In the mind of a child
is a measure of mystery.
The narrative begins before the hour.

It may end at any time.
When he and she meet
never can it be too late.

NEW YEAR

A hollow welcome at an early hour.
The track we find is the one behind
when the textures change,
and meanings enliven the winter
from a lost conclusion.
What approaches is written
in an inventory of spring.
Not every word is legible
to an emerging hunger.
All the days begin again
in deference to the seasons
turning and returning,
a world encircled by time.
Custom accepts this plea for living.

AN OPEN MIND

To hear the morning song
rise with an opening mind
to see the tears of innocence
take root where they will fall.
Nothing so cold it has no life
to feel the growth of the heart
beating in measured steps
across a glistening surface.
What is not ice is water.
Such truth surrounds our world.

Consider then how the leaves are
found in a scattered pattern
as random as the traces of rain.
Reading the leaves reveals the tree
that guards the forest dark
in its deepest secrecy.
So many fingers plough the soil
moving through each stage of wisdom.
In the wellspring of our native tongue
speaks another mind of knowing.

SPEAK AGAIN

History's habit is to rewrite itself
in translation gifted in memory.
We are the future imagined,
becoming the half-remembered past,
only to speak again.
No denial hides the grace
of remaining where we are.

And stones in their dreams
may return to the quarry
where once they rested.
We share with the stones
a way of reading the unwritten
spoken so softly,
becoming the sound in the stones.

WEAVING

As if for a future arrangement
of the craft of the web
the customs are clearly observed.
The spider is given to open display,
freely dancing to a deadly end
in a serious game of weaving
where creatures are cleverly caught.
To the incautious intruder
it is a defence of territory
that is of course a trespass
in what may seem a vacant space.
There will be a crime to confess.

THE HONEY SPOON

Radical Hope
How large is your hand
to hold the world to the light?
How long is the shadow behind?
What follows is sure to be well.

A hint of the original is all
we need to relive the generous days,
our tongues on the honey spoon,
our fingers in the jar of fortune.

Radical Fear
The restoration is played as comedy.
All else is a goosestep away.
Admitting to no principle,
the pragmatic leader acts alone.

A cat is caught in the glare.
Alert to the danger, it is lightning.
The trial begins with an execution,
and 'justice' is served cold.

EVERYONE IS LOOKING

Everyone is looking for everyone else,
hoping to heal the wound
from where the springs of wishes flow
in the manner of a rumour.

This is a city of suggestions,
its influence expanding,
sometimes dreamed, then reasoned
with a silent curiosity
that an observant child inherits.
Slowly the ancient city speaks,
revealing a secret wisdom
from deep within its heart,
the foundation of many lives,
the lost, the lonely and the loved.

FINDING THE WORDS

When the night is calm,
and distant is a reflection
so still it resembles glass.
And no more can be seen
of the lantern in your hand.
It burns with the life of a mayfly
dancing in the water of the pool.
The fragility is the attraction.
Elsewhere in this wilderness
a bottle is floating in the stream,
a galleon on uncharted seas.

Mutiny drifts through the air.
Though there are no words,
their suggestion raises a storm.
The message is clear:
there will be turbulence before landfall.
As rain clouds darkly gather
the words that explain seek release
from a narrow chamber's confinement.
Something escapes into the ether,
no more than a rumour
crossing the threshold of meaning,
Words are sure to follow,
their life sentence served.

A CATCHWORD FOR BEDLAM

Bedlam *The hospital of St Mary of Bethlehem. By extension: A lunatic asylum, a madhouse.*
Oxford English Dictionary 1884

The word is never found now,
full of, or fraught in, mysteries,
difficult to explain, solve or discover.
What an amazing power in writing,
dependant on the phases of the moon.
The sensible sign having few possessions:
the first word of the following page,
the issue of a complication
so placed to catch the eye
before the last line in current language
for the reception and cure of lunatics
under the protection of the city.

THE OTHER COUNTRY

So near us, the other country,
that we might cross unknowingly
though we have no permission,
therefore no right of return
even in sight of homeland,
As a stone disturb s water
so the wall we pass opens
when we walk alone.
Soon we become unseen, speaking
in the trees, in the earth, in the air.

HOW COULD IT BE OTHER?

What may happen next are no more
than suggestions of yours,
one on another foretold
too soon to be believed.
All the words fall like cards
in slow descent to disorder.
The arrangement is agreed
in advance of any advantage.
You follow the idea, no doubt,
when the secret is well hidden?
How could it be other
without betraying our confidence
in all that is sure to be?

A POSSIBLE ANSWER

Your hand grasps a possible answer
though there remains another question.
What is seen is clear
when the entry is opening
to warm the heart of an exile returned.

We stand before the city gate
What is said is heard and felt
so well it is visible.
We are eager to learn
the secret revealed too late
to mark the certainty
when anyone can be sure.

If perception discovers a common cause
there is a union of assurance
beneath the celestial canopy.
The prospect is a lifetime's length
with the desire to begin again.
Beyond our exchange of solitudes
all is fragmented
until all is forgiven.

READING WISDOM

Reading age-old wisdom
is new wine in an old bottle
poured by the hands of mercy
that opens another door,
one that was never there,
and all was a blank wall.

The pages are as virgin snow.
When there are footnotes to follow.
the metaphors are arresting
even in their antiquity.
The sun and stars are favoured
when the moon rests its case,
and the snow falls on summer lawns,
a sure sign of impending war.
The book is closed by common consent.
The age of wisdom is slow to return.

OR THIS PERHAPS

There is rain in the sun
but day will drive the despair
through centuries of metaphor
of a rising time, a moving.
The sycamore speaks discreetly
to advantaged eyes
No doubt dare linger,
a desire to lighten the wold,
The living word runs
towards a shaded space.
At sunset the timely dance
springs from flower to green leaf
with no thought of purpose.
If heard before nightfall
where all is unsettling.
The advice is from exile,
a distant voice calling,
a perpetual shimmering of insight
to keep enquiring minds level.
Another time than this perhaps.

WHEAL JANE

Lives lived in the dark
have eyes now for the sun.
What was drawn from the depths
returns to its source
when bones bless the soil.
Spirits rise with the winding
even in the ruins of history.
And time takes control
until another trajectory
seeks a perpetual season.
Eager hands are hovering
over the remains of many generations.
In the time that may turn
the earth shall move again.

HIDDEN IN LIGHT

The tenderness of the hour
when night is truly timeless
because the darkness dare not
say when morning will come.
Better to trust in candlelight,
the time-honoured guide for travellers
through the inconstant sleeper's dream
when the shape ahead may be spirit
if not a working early riser,
a dawn wanderer in the borderland.
Some say that here is nowhere.
Who can determine when it appears
to be other than everywhere?
There is more truth hidden in light
than in deep darkness,
this rising revelation.

A WEDDING IN ALGHERO

Today there are no sailings to the cape
now summer turns to storm.
The stones of the *viccolo* glisten
in the sunlit squall.
There is shrieking in confusion
towards the island wedding.
Her bridal gown billows,
delicate as the flowering lemons.
She wears innocence proudly.
Life is her paradise.

The old women follow.
Every day they take acceptance
until it becomes their taste.
A priest is prepared in black.
A smile passes his face,
observing how the *campanile*
measures earth against heaven.
Even the rain is a way of seeing
what we love is and shall be.
All things are reflected in the sea.

TANTALUS

The coin spins slowly,
tension tearing at the heart.
Even though the promise is broken
the remains keep their celestial shine,
the judgement being impartial
when a decision is made
as the crystal glass surrenders
to gravity's reckoning.
The coin's purpose is served
for the last, the least of reasons.

Passing through every mood,
an ancestral presence
proved perpetually elusive.
A fly on the window leaps
towards a visible liberty.
But Tantalus is enchained.
Gathered, like dust in the corner,
inquisitive creatures seek
the heart of the world.
Confusion is in the air.

STONE WATER

Owls must haunt the mind,
no wild wanderer dare ignore.
So too with foxes of course.
Ever alert to the power of others,
peaceable creatures gather,
defensive of their territory.

The shiver of the sprinting hare
summons necessity for shelter
from the endless night of winter.
We forget the cleverness of creatures,
ignoring their thoughts,
supposing their sounds make no sense.
We see feathers in flight,
a hurry of startled fur,
without imagining the mind
that goes high or runs with spirit.

The autumnal chill soon falls
on the life of a passing migrant
whose summer's end begins the venture
with the taste of southern sea,
and dust, before a forest sun.
Africa calls its children home.

A transformation declares
its natural intention
to complete the ending of the year.
All life makes to prepare.

Ice begins its sharp descent,
as clear as lovers' innocence
betrayed by cynical frost
when water is stilled in its course.
In winter there is only stone;
no feather, no fur, no bone.

SUNFLOWER

Time has turned the pages
to the colour of the sun
setting in the winter haze.
A caged bird's feather floats
into mind when light fades
on the flesh of aged faces
with the texture of wrinkled parchment.

The aroma of jasmine vanishes
when the world fears the worst
in the drifting cloud of desert dust.
And the taste of lemons
is a sharper sign of war.
A ribbon of remembrance cries
for a sowing of the sunflower.

COUNTING THE HOURS

Counting the hours
as they speed the day
that is always passing.

A night may be measured in candlewax,
daylight by the pattern of shadows
in the progress of the sun.

What is spoken of this
tends towards song.
The rhythm is natural.
The motion has no end
because the song has no end
that a mind can conjecture.

What begins with harmony
in the shape of a sphere.
ends with ice, with fire.

TO THE ARC APPEARING

Leaves this year are late in falling
because of the trees in their watering.
The fields, unharvested, are full.
To Genesis again
a child draws the Flood
as animals gather in her mind.
The apple returns to the earth
on which a faith in life floats.
We are creatures of the deep.
All that will continue comes
to the arc appearing
in dreams that wake her,
graceful in every aspect,
unknowing of the dangers
written with her in mind.
What a word can do with a life inside
searching the world for meaning.

WHILE SUMMER LASTS

Then at the equinox no more
the summer's music plays.
While summer lasts there is song
in a sweeter air than winter's blast.
Especially at the day's fading,
a relief from hot, dry dust
and the yellowing of the green
anticipating rainfall.
Earth is in cultivation
piled high in the season's turn,
sustaining marvellous plenty,
a mercy gathered where it may
grow beyond the bounds
of any season's span.

A HOLY HINT

The Blackbird's Song

To say how is my love
will you fly to her
on silken wings,
bird of silver song
with your sweet tongue?

One or two or three things
are never easy to find:
counting the stars in the frost,
or touching the moon,
or hearing the mind of my love.

CLEY-NEXT-THE-SEA

A long strand of stones
saltwater washed.
The wind among the reeds
carries many desires
from sea to sky, featherlight.
Ghost music drifting through
new channels and ancient ways
of water, land and waterland.
The sea shall swallow the stones.
It is only a matter of time.

SO MUCH WE SAY

An apple in the orchard ripens
ready to be taken as the fruit
of a natural curiosity
for available desires
that entice our innocence..
Then is the matter of invention
on the earth in motion.
The bones of history
engendered in the wild
now feel tamed by human toil.
Suffering seeks the mercy
of Providence coming and going.

There are voices close and clear
from a cluster of utterances
echoing in a growing awareness.
Meaning is likely to be found
in signs of understanding.
There may be love in this
when lips part with promises.
These thoughts are written with silence
I take care not to spill.
There are ways of saying well
what no-one wants to hear.
So much we say is silence.

THE HOLKHAM GEESE

The geese must feed upon
a cycle of sacrifice
from their growth in silence
to the harvest hour.
Furrow by furrow the earth moving
the land yields its riches slowly.
Survival follows the plough
for signs for any vital offerings.
A goose must cast a curious eye,
the horizon never being far away
in the search across many seas
for life beneath a wing's shadow.

But the trees hide their secret well,
whereas the open land invites.
And here is a haven
found in an ambient season,
a time of contentment.
Of this discovery the geese must sing.

THE SUN DOES NOT RISE

To observe from the vantage of the stars
our days on earth live to see new worlds rising
when this world feels weightless
in an angel's hand.
There is the sun in splendour
yet we can never hold the light,
a failing to see how we are
when we are for certain there.

The sun does not rise,
but we are the ones who move
with the turnaround world
turning again to lose the sun.
The falling is also ours.

THERE IS A LIFE

Lights in the night sky shine in her eyes.
Then into the world she makes
what comes to life in her mind
smiling at the thought of every enigma
These things she has yet to see.
her feast an invitation to the sacred
truth that may be found in unlikely places.
Where else, she wonders, would it be?
The question is open to every answer,
and truth is evident in the maker's mind.

Consider her vision.
Observations are quickened into life
where the connections spiral,
the imagined flight of mechanical birds.
She has set the scene in her reality.
The tangible vision is all,
with a charming discretion
or outrageous denial
of what surely makes sense.

There is a life waiting to be born.
Her dreams are taken on trust,
their images so exquisite,
A reflection of the world to come,
if only by inference,'
she explains to an idle apprentice.
Creation begins with a word
containing all that can be known,

all that moves with the sun.
It is her child in the womb.
A new world is at hand.

THE TRUTH ON THE TONGUE

The truth is not yet in sight,
nothing to be seen by human eyes.
In a room where there is no-one
every sound resonates,
the pulse of time perhaps,
or the scurrying of fear.

Not every truth is well told.
The stain may be mistaken
for blood's embittered rage
in a shattering and a scattering.
The glass in your hand contains the wine
that holds the truth on every tongue.

Words loosened from care
come rolling down the hill
until they touch reality
that is an empty glass.

A VIEW OF EVERYTHING

Beyond this room are more rooms
reflected in the eyes of the world.
And all other things begin
where the curiosity ends.
At a casual glance we see
a sudden transformation
with no evidence denied.
Here we have a view of everything
that our hearts dare keep in mind
as we look through a visible space.
This we aim to remember,
and so try to avoid
what may be nothing at all.
The room in mind is open.

LISTENING TO THE STONES

Listening to the stones as they roll,
a motion that has no end
to impede the momentum,
a bringing of style to life.
Such incandescence compels,
burning in the fire of perpetual youth.
A destiny is determined by the rhythm,
a feeling no-one has felt before.
That is a fever of the new.
In their quest for ecstasy
sensation-seekers assemble,
making thunder in the streets,
a spirit to live inside the sound
so powerful it shakes the walls.
As for the stones, they are old,
but their power does no fade.

ANCIENT & MODERN

A river flows down from the sky,
its course clear and purposeful,
a cascade of the sacred.
If lightning's profanity follows
dismissal is a ready response.
An echo of prayer in the quire
is inspiration seeking endeavour.

*

Second by second into the future
history is made here
along the narrow lane.
A pause to listen for a moment
when footsteps falter in passing.
Voices are rehearsing
what will become harmony
from a curious cacophony.

*

Opening the King's Arms,
she returns the key to her coat.
It is almost noon, and a bell tolls
for another hour passing
and the morning swept away.
There is thirst in the air,
a quickening pace at the thought.
Her task is to serve their sad revels

until the time to be herself comes again.
For some this is everything

*

In low light a quiet withdrawal
from life's illusory surface
wherein simplicity glides.
A pale countenance considers
how the light lets shadows dance
when suddenly a lantern swings.
The scriptorium creaks like a ship's timbers.
All that is not flesh is wood
or ink or vellum or parchment.
The world of time's turning is stilled.

ON THE WILD HILL

Sometimes in the sun,
choosing a hidden shade
revealed by chance exploration
of the farther margins,
a rose graces the tangled growth
unplanned and free to be
the surprise of existence,
the purpose of generation.

A universe of life in the wound
of a tree felled, rotting,
yet in decay a plenitude
of harboured creation dancing
as it feeds on this accidence,
and in turn is eaten.
The pattern is circular,
giving another life to rise.

ON THE FALLEN

The surprise has all the signs
of the entirely predictable
when citizens are shocked and speechless
in the face of the firestorm.
Good sense sleeps in the heat
then shaken by the betrayal
of nature and her graces.
A dry dust settles on the fallen.
The world moves out of reason
as a warning too late to be heard.
So like Chaplin falling,
the dried, decaying leaves define the spring.

AN ARTIST PREPARES

This thought serves me well
in a style reflecting simply what is.
The change perpetual is named
though rarely with ease.
The vision commits itself to art.
Beneath the surface possession
every version differs in detail,
those barely visible signs
of life, my lady, before it happens
where there was an encompassing void.

When the fear of mystery overwhelms
the material mind of the world
the unexplained may disappear
only to return in other ways.

The day is diamantine,
a casual grace adorning the world.
when portrayed in the venture
of a canvas so prepared.
It is for this that sleepers wake
shedding the skin of night
as mere brocade, now faded.
What cannot be seen is real.

The surest way is to touch.
When a finger explores the wound
then faith follows, eyes closed
in a walking dream

that conjures colour and shape.
These are familiar to me.
I am accused by some of sorcery,
and cursed by those envious of gifts
that are mine by the grace of chance.
Consider it as prayer, my lady.

LIONESS & CHAMPION

Life is always in motion
with her pride rising
because the scene is changing
between the acts of timelessness.
The lioness devours all beauty
held by the champion's hand
in another history unwritten
of secrets never to be shared.

The souls of the lost seek rest
as embers from the beacon burn
if only by speculation
on the inequity of the law.
Hovering in lonely judgement
sings the stinging fly.
These things are known to be
star-like tears glistening

JAUFRE RUDEL

Le chanson du rossignol
qui Rudel adore.
la reine angélique d'Afrique
avec un merveilleux aubade.
L'amour est une affaire
dans le nuit espérant
vers le côte d'Outremer
après un voyage pacifique.
Enfin un mouillage tranquille
ici le soleil couche sous la mer
comme un somnambule qui parle
son amour parfait.

Rudel sang of the nightingale,
all the while admiring her,
angelic queen of darkness
and wakening enchantments.
The meaning is in love,
a romance of night's intimations
in sight of a Levantine shore
on a calm, cool crossing
that ends in quiet anchorage.
Here the sunset articulates
the somnambulance of dying
within reach of love's embassy.

MIRAGE

Something else is seen
from a fissure in the stone.
What must never pass
is mistaking the echo for the voice,
or a reflection in the glass
for the living presence,
the spirit in the matter.

The simplicity you seek shimmers
in your accepting eye
deceived by appearance too easily.
A mirage to mock the world.
A response will be revealed
in tracing the source.
Like desire it is wild of course
and no less labyrinthine
in its closures and openings
on the way to the heart
All is clear, all that you are.

'TEMPTESTUOUS' SEAS

An Imagined Memory

Not everyone we know lives
in the way others suppose.
The palest of presences
are visible in the air about us,
like an unborn sister
whose eyes have never opened.
All about her is conjecture,
a life in many directions
all leading to the vacant room
echoing the charm of her.

The portrait we make of her changes
to a lovelier she year by year.
The style suits each mood and moment,
always alert to her situation.
Lively, she was known to turn wild.
A sudden fury could sting
with tears of rage at the torment.
She was too easily hurt by life.
Yet this life we were denied.
Her absence has been ours.

*

We see her stand there, watching.
What might have been is history.
that will not be written readily.

Endeavour will find a way
that is both blessing and curse.

*

The air was unusually clear,
and all haze strangely erased
until the storm swept over the land.
No more dancing in the rain,
we sheltered in our memories.
When some girls at school sang
of *'temptestuous'* seas
the word they made had truth there.
I wonder what song they sing now.
One voice alone sings so well.

THE SADNESS OF NAMES

A bell sounds for an end
of another day whose life is done.
There need be no fear in faith
that is almost visible,
or so the air suggests.

Some will pass on the other side
from the old churchyard wall,
especially at low light
when thought must turn to others
in the sounding of spirit,

This is the time of prayer,
a summoning of reflections
on the almost forgotten
among the sadness of names
carved, enclosed, lived in stone.

EVERYTHING STILL MOVES

An alarm wakes the sleeping guard.
There is a fire to burn the world down.
What is unsaid is testament
to all that is yet to be.
The old enemy appears.

Rivers of ice, fields of frost.
No-one dare cross the cold line
in the narrow void
that opens up as ocean-wide
when the journey has no departure.
The wall echoes discarded lives.
All words in war are of conflict.

Were it to leap from the tree
a quizzical cat might answer
if only to see what we are
who seek our better selves.
Nothing can ever be certain.

The bridge of many crossings
sways with history
above the abyss
mistaken for peace
by desperate believers.
As we make our way over
a barrier betrays expectations.
The standing stones are moving,
tired of their silence

in the millennia of human war
which they have witnessed with pity,
powerless to intervene
The stones have led a life apart,
but now they are speaking
no longer in contemplation.
We hear unearthly sounds
in the wilder places
where our lost hopes have wandered
only to find everything still moves

To wake again in Byzantium
when all the centuries surrender
to the shadow of antiquity.
A life spans but one stream
that springs from the mind.
Within the bounds someone is seen
whose presence nobody can explain.
Evading capture, she will not leave.
Be sure, she says, the water is pure,
cool to touch, sweet to taste.
By the waters of paradise
our souls lie down at last.

THOSE ANCIENT PLACES

Once there lived thoughts
that grew from the groundswell
of natural chances.
In time they became timber
and the trees that lined the road,
spread through diverse avenues
Rivers were bridged, and fine life flowed.
Houses were framed to endure.
When citizens were of one view
they made their way together.
Those ancient places found their way
from dream to life that lived.

FLOATING

Marking the steps you take,
the cracks in the ground testify
to the years the city has seen.
A long line of aspiration
is leaving you breathless at the end
that is also an arrival.

You tread a paradox walking
on the old, uneven road.
Some suppose it an obstacle
as they stagger and stumble
on their way that is sure to be down
because they do not see you rise.

To a lighter tune you dance.
At times the music moves
anticipating a change of mood
that comes and then goes,
like clouds in a clear sky,
or a crowd in a lonely street.
Floating, you view the scene below
before your higher ascent begins.

OF STYLE WITH MEANING

The voice is long in sadness
all of loss learned by heart.
The appeal is spoken so well
it compels the ear to open.
Everything could be perhaps
in the first draft of time,
hearing how easily he speaks the line
of style with meaning,

A delicate flower grows in finer soil.
The passage is taken back.
There will be another time
always in anticipation
of a defined design in rhythm.
Something finds its way there,
a seeking of sanctuary
that returns in time to source.

AN ECLIPSE FORETELLS

An unsettling stillness is falling
on a world devoured
when all about is absence
through the fading of the light.
For someone whose eyes must close
there is no song in the air,
nor sun rising in the soul.
An eclipse foretells the end
we are never able to evade
by hope of signs in the sky.
What do we see in the void?
Perhaps our lives can touch the stars,
and so we have eyes to open
to believe in the marvels
that those below cannot see
when the light sings again.

THE DOOR WHERE WE CAME IN

Shared like a secret insight
we view the house as living
in union with our lives.
The kitchen is more than a cooking room,
and the garden an abundance
of nurtured growth with colour
and all the aromas of growth.
What is fed in turn feeds us.
Fruit flowers, ripens, then falls
reflecting the process
of everything that lives
when time's shadow eclipses the sun.
These things of nature are known,
only to be lost in transition,
the crisis in our command
of where we make habitation.
We grow season by season,
our lives lasting for ever
until the never of leaving
by the door where we came in.

EYES CLOSED

Standing like an ancient stone.
Waiting like an open gate.
What purpose do metaphors serve
but to make words sound well
and so profound that heaven may spring
from the impacted earth of the track?.
The answer masquerades as the question:
What shall I see when all is invisible?

NOTES

The acts of writing and reading are forms of reliving. We draw upon our experiences when we write. We bring something of our experience into our reception of a creative work. We filter the words through our archive of personal memory.

What lurks in the shadow but a window?

'Long overdue,' was one reviewer's comment on my first collection. It came about due to the exceptional kindness of an invitation. Both the invitation and the critical praise were surely signs of grace in which a secular age does not believe. It is unfashionable to speak of ANGELS. A guiding hand is always there. I am not writing the poem alone. I am fortunate to share my undeserved wealth.

JAUFRE RUDEL: Neither version is a translation of the other.

Rudel, troubadour of medieval Provence, travelled to the Holy Land. His poetry was written in Occitan, the traditional language of Provence, still spoken today. It was poetry with music, and sung in the courts of love where troubadours had their work judged by presiding ladies.

Jaufre is Occitan (the traditional language of Provence) for Geoffrey. Jaufre Rudel voyaged to meet the Countess of Tripoli. He collapsed as the ship approached the Levantine shore. He died in the arms of the Countess whom he had hoped to love.

WHEAL JANE was a tin mine in Kernow/Cornwall. Tin mining in the peninsula dates back to antiquity. The last mine closed in 1998, but there is the possibility of a revival. Tin mining was a hard life well described in A.L. Rowse's *A Cornish Childhood*.

A HOLY HINT is freely adapted from a traditional Welsh poem

www.ingramcontent.com/pod-product-compliance
Ingram Content Group UK Ltd.
Pitfield, Milton Keynes, MK11 3LW, UK
UKHW041316190726
13845UKWH00025B/312

9 789363 548534